THE Southern
RUSTIC CABIN

THE Southern RUSTIC CABIN

EMILY J. FOLLOWILL

with Lisa Frederick

GIBBS SMITH
TO ENRICH AND INSPIRE HUMANKIND

In memory of dear Dad.
He and his endearing love, Southern grace,
and devotion to the land and people in the South
were with me every step of this adventure.

———

To Tom, Sarah, and Thomas,
you are my world!

19 18 17 16 15   5 4 3 2 1

Photographs © 2015 Emily J. Followill
Text © 2015 Lisa Frederick

Published by
Gibbs Smith
P.O. Box 667
Layton, Utah 84041

1.800.835.4993 orders
www.gibbs-smith.com

Designed by Katie Jennings Campbell
Pages produced by Melissa Dymock
Printed and bound in Hong Kong

Gibbs Smith books are printed on either recycled,
100% post-consumer waste, FSC-certified papers
or on paper produced from a 100% certified
sustainable forest/controlled wood source.

Library of Congress Cataloging-in-Publication Data

Followill, Emily.
  The Southern rustic cabin / Emily J. Followill ;
with Lisa Frederick. — First Edition.
      pages cm
  ISBN 978-1-4236-3885-8
1. Log cabins—Southern States. 2. Decoration and
ornament, Rustic—Southern States. I. Title.
  NA8470.F65 2015
  728.7'30975—dc23
                                                    2015008006

CONTENTS

ACKNOWLEDGMENTS

To all the people who were instrumental and helpful in making this happen, I appreciate each of you and your contribution.

Thank you to the assistants and friends that helped carry the load on the road and in the homes: Kathryn Rogers, Andrew Horne, Kelly Blackmon, Samantha Angel, Lacey Sombar, and Andrea Dorsey. You are all dear friends and are always ready to go the extra mile for the shot. Thank you also to Kyle Burdg for putting the finishing touch on many of these images, and to Eleanor Roper and Lisa Mowry for putting your stylistic touch and beautiful props and flowers in some of the cabins.

I truly enjoyed the people I met while on the road, and was delighted to stay in the project areas. Thank you to Tom and Mary Katherine Greene for giving me the key to your wonderful home in the North Carolina mountains and for your scouting assistance on those winding roads!

Thank you, Lisa Frederick, for your words, which bring the photographs to life and tell the story of each cabin. You truly took the project under your wing and used great care to interview everyone involved to retell their stories for you. I am so thankful for your gift with words.

Maggie Kennedy, Photography Director at *Garden and Gun* magazine, you were an enormous help. When I asked to pick your brain about log cabins in the South, you immediately came up with several homes, which were great additions to the book. Many thanks for brainstorming with me.

James Farmer, thank you for introducing me to my editor, Madge Baird, at Gibbs Smith. James, you are an amazing talent, and it is through working with you that this book evolved. This would not have been possible without you. I'm thankful for your unending joy in all that you do. Madge, you have been a patient and faithful tour guide and mentor on this fun adventure. Thank you for your knowledge and advice, and for making it a delightful process.

Most of all, I thank my incredible family. To my mother, thank you for always lending a patient ear, encouraging me every step of the way, being a wonderful and helpful grandmother, and being the best mother I could ask for. As we know, it will all work out! Your unending strength, love, and compassion never go unnoticed. Ann Carol and Judge, thank you for being wonderful parents-in-law, loving and supporting me at all times. Your cabin is a beautiful southern rustic retreat that delights all of us. And to my children, thank you for being you. I am incredibly blessed to be your mom. Thank you for your patience while I was away from home. You always welcomed me home with hugs and kisses that meant the world to me after a long day of work and travel. I hope you know that you can be whatever you want to be with Christ by your side.

To Tom, you know that none of this would be possible without you as my rock, my sounding board, my rational side, my love, my Christian companion, and my dearest friend. I love you.

Finally, thank you to the reader. I hope you will find this book a wonderful retreat in itself.

FOREWORD

Southern and rustic: these two words are as congruent as mossy rocks in a cool mountain stream.

The South is a land of complementary combinations; a land whose cadence and rhythm is dedicated to the balancing harmony that a juxtaposition of opposites affords. We eat our homegrown, earthy garden delights and fried catfish, too, on precious heirloom plates on which our grandmothers hand-painted their monograms with delicate silver. In college, we attend tailgates and football games in our finest Sunday attire. We build fine homes painted a gleaming white, with columns and parapets and porches extending into the red clay and loamy farmland. As a people, we celebrate our heritage—our homeland that is likewise a mélange of peoples who share this patchwork of coastal marshes, fertile deltas, rolling farms, peach- and pecan-lined fields and ancient mountain ridges.

It is in these ancient mountains that we southerners find solace from the summer heat that their altitude affords. Here we can experience true seasons, not simply "hot and not-so-hot." Here, though, amid the granite cliffs, oak-cloaked ridges and waterfall-laced Appalachian Mountains we find congruence with nature again—not our southerly juxtaposition of opposites. In Appalachia and the foothills and into the surrounding lands, we find log cabins—southern and rustic—constructed of hand-felled and -hewn logs from the rocky ridges. Along with the logs are the cedar shakes, pine boards, laurel wood railings and chestnut bark siding, all of which play into the reverence southern cabins pay to their setting.

Our log cabins are our home places and retreats, where we raise families, summer, or simply escape for tranquility amid summer's feverish heat. These homes are the scenes for reflecting on nature amidst nature itself in a home clad with treasured trees. This is where we can be southern and rustic—not southern and sophisticated, with our balancing acts of silver julep cups and barbeque. That balance, though, is who we are and a hallmark of our famous hospitality. When the time comes for us to be southern and rustic, that, y'all, is never more apropos than in our log cabin homes amidst our hallowed, beloved mountains and farms.

—*James T. Farmer III*
author of *A Time to Plant, A Time to Cook*
and *Dinner on the Grounds;*
editor-at-large, *Southern Living*

INTRODUCTION

"The quiet rhythmic monotone of the wall of logs fills one with the rustic peace of a secluded nook in the woods." —GUSTAV STICKLEY

I was born in the South. It's where my parents were born. It's where my grandparents were born. It's where I went to school. It's where my husband was born, and it's where his family was born. It's where my children were born. It always has been, and will be, a part of who I am. If you were to ask me where my heart belongs, it's not hard to imagine how I would respond.

The South is defined by its beautiful countryside, its rustic origins, and its people's creativity. It is a beautiful area of the country in which to live, work, and play. When it is time to relax, my ideal place to retreat from everyday life is nature. Time spent in a cabin in the woods, on a mountain, or by a lake is a true vacation for me. Of course, the creature comforts are wonderful, but it's the place that moves me and allows me to rest, relax, and restore. It was with this in mind that I was inspired to capture the southern feeling through the architecture and design of some of the South's most wonderful log cabins.

"Keep close to Nature's heart . . . and break clear away, once in awhile, and climb a mountain or spend a week in the woods. Wash your spirit clean." —John Muir

The South is blessed with rustic homes, and you would be hard-pressed to find someone who doesn't know of one nearby. Some were built hundreds of years ago and some last week, and still others incorporate an incredible blend of old and new. A few of the older homes have been restored inside and out to the simplicity of years ago, while others have the most modern conveniences. Regardless, the ingenuity and creative talents required to design and redesign these rustic spaces is special. Whether it's a quaint one-bedroom cottage or a larger mountain retreat that can welcome the extended family for Thanksgiving, cabins all remind us of comfort, safety, and a sense of warmth. It is my hope that you will feel this as you witness the incredible work of the architects, designers, and, of course, the homeowners captured in these pages.

"If you would know strength and patience, welcome the company of trees." —HAL BORLAND

As I traveled the South to each of these retreats, it was almost as if I was on a treasure hunt. My GPS might get me close to the cabin, but I often needed extra directions to get me all the way there. At the end of a winding road, I was so excited to round the last curve and see the jewel come into view. The experiences were matched by the enjoyment of learning its origin and meeting the people who helped it come to life. It was delightful to watch the story of each cabin unfold as I worked.

At each home I was warmly welcomed by someone involved in the process of the cabin—homeowner, interior designer, architect, or caretaker. After hearing the cabin's story, I was left to experience and record the home as I saw it. That trust assured me that these homes were created as much for their guests to enjoy as for the homeowners.

I hope you enjoy this peek into and around thirteen log homes in the South. It has been a true blessing to capture all of these images.

BORN *to* BUILD

— HENDERSONVILLE, TENNESSEE —

Maryanna Dixon had never believed in love at first sight until it happened to her. Twice.

The house started it. Built for Johnny Cash, who had deeded it to his daughter Cindy and then-son-in-law Marty Stuart, it was a melting pot of indigenous woods and salvaged curios in the hills on the fringe of Nashville. It had piqued Maryanna's interest when she got wind, from her home in New York City, that it was for sale. She flew down to see the place and bought it on the spot.

"It was something that I felt about this house—something indescribable," says Maryanna, a cabaret singer who has toured all over the world. Little did she know where that feeling would lead. After she arrived, as she was elbow-deep in boxes, "in walks this good-looking man, and he puts his arms around me and says, 'Welcome to the hill.' I fell in love with him the second I saw him."

"This good-looking man" was Braxton Dixon, a master builder who builds for future country music royalty as comfortably as he wields a trowel. Now in his nineties, he's a legend, renowned for his singular approach to construction. He blends time-honored methods with centuries-old materials that he sources by hand, canvassing the country for antique stained

glass, architectural fragments, ephemera—anything that speaks to his impeccable eye for detail.

Braxton's talent is inborn, as pure as the stones from which he built his first house at the age of fourteen. As a toddler, he would crawl around to pick up blocks that his father, a carpenter, sawed off the ends of red cedar. It was in his mind, heart, and soul from the very beginning.

Braxton, who has handcrafted just over fifty houses through the years, is famous for the care he lavishes on every last element. "No new material ever goes into his houses. He hasn't bought a new piece of wood in sixty-five years," says Maryanna.

It's no surprise, then, that the Dixons have surrounded themselves with homes rooted in the past. The six cabins on their Hendersonville property, known as Sycamore Homestead, date as far back as 1789. Of them all, the guesthouse known as Mud Lick House is the most authentic as far as being handmade. Built in

‹ The house that Maryanna Dixon (then Maryanna McConnell) bought before meeting Braxton, the master builder who would become her husband, was the first cabin on their property, Sycamore Homestead. They have since added five more.

⌐ The large wheel on this porch at the Mud Lick House once belonged to Johnny Cash, who used to store his guns between the spokes. In front stands an old train-wheel cog mold from a rail yard.

∧ An 1890s corbel from a Victorian home in Kentucky, which Braxton dismantled, frames this porch. Its twin is mounted on the opposite side of the house.

❯ Braxton integrated two Roman chariot wheels into the decorative screen that fronts the Mud Lick House's side porch. The wheels were shipped over by a group of men whom he befriended in Italy during his service in World War II.

Born to Build

1800 alongside a creek in Mud Lick, Kentucky, the cabin caught Braxton's fancy as soon as he spotted it.

It was the greatest log house he had ever seen—a full two stories but only seven logs high (most are twelve to thirteen). The massive poplar logs had been gathered from the site on which the cabin stood. It took a long time, but he eventually convinced the owner, a descendant of the pioneer who constructed Mud Lick House, to sell it.

Braxton spent the next twenty-plus years rehabilitating the cabin piece by painstaking piece. He laid a kitchen floor in a pattern of overlapping squares, using precious wood he'd saved for six decades. He designed and built a free-hanging staircase and erected an enormous living room fireplace of hand-cut 19th-century Tennessee limestone.

Although a Braxton Dixon house is unmistakable, there are two signatures that mark each one indelibly as his. One began by chance. After a night of carousing with his older friends, a sluggish Braxton was helping his father top off a stone chimney. "His father said, 'Son, I'm going to get some rock dust, and while I'm gone, try to put your heart in your work,'" Maryanna says. Braxton happened to look down and see a piece of sandstone shaped like a heart. When his dad saw it, he said, "What the dad-gum is that?" Braxton said, "Well, Daddy, you told me to put my heart in it." Since then, every chimney he's built has included a heart atop the stones.

∧ This 1789 Tennessee smokehouse, the oldest structure at Sycamore Homestead, is now Maryanna's garden house. An antique log turner, once used to transport logs, hangs alongside the door.

⟩ The Dixons' most historically important treasures went into the Mud Lick House. The main door once was part of a home belonging to Andrew Jackson's law partner. Above it hangs a tinwork panel salvaged from a Nashville bank.

The other signature element is a cross, embedded somewhere amid the wood surfaces in each home. It's sometimes obvious, sometimes not. But no matter where it appears, Maryanna says, the underlying message is the same: "His gift is God-given."

⌐ Braxton laid every stone in the eight-foot-wide fireplace by himself. The hearthstone, which weighs half a ton, had to be brought in by crane.

‹ A few specimens from Braxton's collection of hundreds of antique locks and keys hang on the wall.

› This cast-iron Victorian light fixture, which has four kerosene fonts, came from a country church that Braxton saw being demolished near Pulaski, Tennessee. He gave the bulldozer driver $10 in exchange for a few minutes to salvage the fixture.

Born to Build

« The Dixons' collection of rare finds includes this hand-carved mantel, depicting an urn atop a law book.

‹ A piece of stone found in the original chimney of the Mud Lick House is carved with the exact year the home was built.

‹ Braxton always includes a piece of stained glass in each of his homes. These matching windows were salvaged from a town outside St. Louis through which Braxton passed on his travels.

› The mirror in the Mud Lick House bathroom is from an old washstand; the sink was retrofitted from a porcelain washstand bowl.

<< Braxton made the dining table base from an old loom. The top is cut down from a single piece of wood once used for slaughtering hogs. Steel strips around the edge prevent the wood from expanding.

< A copper vessel from a Nashville candy factory was transformed into the kitchen sink. Instead of traditional spigots, a spout that was formerly part of an old pitcher hand pump extends from the wall. Foot pedals control the flow of hot and cold water.

^ The overlapping boards that comprise the kitchen floor are made from the ten indigenous fruit and nut tree species that grow on the Dixons' hill. A hand-painted chicken tile sits at the center.

Born to Build

∧ Carved from solid stone in Carrara, Italy, this bathtub was shipped over by the same group of men who sent the chariot wheels. Its glaze represents the era when this technique was first perfected.

❯ This bedroom, which was originally part of the porch, features solid cedar flooring and 200-year-old windows on either side of the bed. Antique children's school chairs stand in for traditional night tables.

CULTIVATING MEMORIES

— MADISON, GEORGIA —

Like so many restoration projects, this one started small. Thirty-plus years ago, Atlantans Carolyn and John Malone bought a spread of acreage in Madison, Georgia, with an eye toward turning the former cow pasture into a landscape nursery.

They needed somewhere to sleep during their weekend forays to the property, but were on the fence about what form it would take. Enter a chance find in the Atlanta newspaper: an advertisement that listed an 1840s log cabin in Summer Shade, Kentucky. Intrigued, the Malones headed up to north Georgia to meet with the broker. A glance through his photos was all it took to sell them on the place. Thus began a labor of love that eventually would extend to three more nineteenth-century cabins with Deep South roots, transported to the compound that the couple named Summershade, in honor of the flagship structure.

"Once we got the first cabin finished, we knew we wanted to restore more," says Carolyn, an interior designer known for her neutral, fuss-free style. "It was their unmanufactured quality, the hand-hewn logs and timbers. They have a kind of humble beauty."

Beauty aside, all four buildings needed serious rehabilitation. They came as a pile of logs. With construction help from neighbors, Carolyn and John rolled up their sleeves and dug in. The second cabin they purchased became a kitchen; the third, which had once been a dogtrot, became guest quarters; and the fourth was integrated with the main house as a bar and bathroom. The couple added shake roofs in keeping with the cabins' era, and clad the interiors in reclaimed flooring and ceiling beams.

Basic systems such as plumbing and wiring were kept as unobtrusive as possible, so as not to mar the sense of age. The Malones also eschewed conveniences such as central heat and air, opting for fans instead. "It's pretty primitive," Carolyn says. "We did the least amount that we could to be comfortable without losing the rusticity."

For John, working on the cabins became a crash course in restoration. He hand-chinked the logs using traditional methods, and crafted windows, doors (hinges included), light fixtures and lanterns, plus the couple's cypress bed. "He's a gifted craftsman and learned as he went," Carolyn says.

Carolyn and John Malone's dog, Dillard, relaxes on the front lawn of first cabin that the couple bought for their property from Summer Shade, Kentucky.

Cultivating Memories

< An Irish fence, with its distinctive crisscrossing design, runs along the grounds.

> The kitchen porch on the Summer Shade cabin overlooks a small pond.

Carolyn's interior scheme adheres to the simple, natural style that a log cabin dictates, with a few dashes of her trademark subdued elegance mixed in. "You don't have a lot of flexibility as to the materials," she explains. "You really can't do a lot of color on the walls because your walls are what they are. That's what I like about them. Logs are a beautiful backdrop, very comforting and quiet."

She preserved that sense of tranquility in the trappings. Nuanced whites, browns and greens dominate the palette, enlivened by big bunches of flowers and baskets of vegetables gathered from outside. Textural fabrics mingle with honed finishes. Simple antiques are layered throughout the rooms, chosen more for their clean lines and storied air than their provenance.

One item in particular is among Carolyn's most special: a vintage pie safe from her home state of Alabama, the first piece she and John bought for the property. It's an apt metaphor for the enduring sense of rootedness that the cabins call to mind. She says, "They're very humble buildings, but beautiful and so strong."

⌐ Confederate jasmine climbs the wall adjacent to the herb and vegetable garden.

❯ An old cabinet serves as a kitchen pantry.

❯❯ The Malones call this small cabin, which was moved to the property from north Georgia, the "nap house."

ꓶ An outdoor shower allows for a quick rinse-off.

ꓶ A stack of kitchen firewood waits for use.

⟩ Faux-bois log planters on the cabin's original front porch add another layer of texture that blends with the rustic woods.

‹ Rock gathered from the fields surrounding the cabin was used to build the chimney. The clock on the mantel is a family heirloom.

^ An antique pie safe from Alabama, the couple's first purchase, stands against one wall.

^ Local art and agricultural drawings are clustered on a wall of the cabin's main room.

∧ The library and office for John's nursery holds his collection of books. Mary Morant, Carolyn's niece, did the painting on the wall.

˥ John made the light fixture from a baling basket. French bee skeps line the shelf above the window.

＞ Stacked locust rails stand in for a fireplace and chimney in this cabin, a former dogtrot. The design allows for generous sunlight.

‹ The kitchen has no cabinetry, only a skirt to conceal its inner workings. A creeping fig has made its home inside.

∧ Kitchen shelving holds a collection of redware bowls and tureens.

› A vintage zinc-top potting table was transformed into a kitchen island.

< A handmade cypress bed has pride of place in the master bedroom. Over the mantel hangs a sand painting of a tree.

> The corner desk holds a Magnolia macrophylla blossom.

> This antique wicker chaise provides a spot for a quiet retreat.

∧ A fruit harvesting bag is among the accents Carolyn sprinkled into the nap house.

˥ Whitewashed walls and flooring give this guestroom an ethereal air. A painting by Atlanta artist Katherine Bell McClure rests on the bench.

› Vintage letters that Carolyn found in North Carolina spell out a message in the nap house.

Overleaf: In the dogtrot guestroom, sconces made from old cheese paddles flank a pencil-post bed.

DREAM HOME COME TRUE

— ELLIJAY, GEORGIA —

As a busy TV producer and interior designer, Brian Patrick Flynn is used to turning projects around on a dime. So it's no surprise that as soon as he closed on his north Georgia log cabin, he didn't waste a moment bringing it up to speed. "About two hours after I signed the papers, I had my remodeling crew ripping out windows," says Brian.

The cabin represents the fulfillment of a longtime dream. Although Brian had promised himself that he'd own a mountain house by his mid-thirties, he hadn't decided just where. As it turned out, the perfect spot was right under his nose: Ellijay, Georgia, a stone's throw north of his Atlanta home. "I didn't know that only an hour and twenty minutes from the city there was this completely different landscape," he says. Smitten with the area, Brian and his partner began scouring Web sites for the ideal cabin. The winner, though, came by happenstance. Driving through the mountains, they spied a house not listed online, tucked at the top of a peak and 20,000 feet from its nearest neighbor. Best of all was the view over the Appalachians, which went on for miles. The minute they opened the door and looked inside, they knew it was the one.

That's not to say that it was *total* love at first sight. The interior was covered in dated yellow pine; the kitchen and bathrooms needed a face-lift; and the tiny windows eclipsed the breathtaking views. Still, the footprint was fantastic, and the couple saw straight through to the cabin's potential for visual drama.

During the whirlwind remodel, the crew replaced doors and the windows with larger models; they installed new ceiling beams and supplanted the old fireplace with a sleek, modern one. Smoothing the transition to the screened-in porch maximized the full 1,400 square feet of outdoor living space—almost as much as in the house itself. The pine walls and floors in the main rooms were unified with a coat of warm white paint, which helps draw the eye to the spectacular foliage outside the windows.

One of the biggest changes the couple made was to paint the exterior in a totally unexpected hue: black. "That was definitely a risk," Brian says, "but it doesn't look morbid; it looks sophisticated." In winter, the cabin makes an arresting contrast with the snow; in warmer weather, it plays well with the surrounding foliage.

Black notes echo throughout the interior as well—most strikingly in a custom stair railing that Brian had crafted for the living room. Slim welded steel bars, powder-coated in a matte black finish, tower along the stairway and make the space appear far bigger than it is.

Although Brian intended for the decor to evoke a sense of place, he also wanted to steer clear of mountain-house clichés. He nixed woodsy finishes and dark metals in favor of large swaths of white, shots of juicy color, and matte brass top notes. Rich navy cloaks a guest bunkroom; others wear persimmon or apple green. Furnishings and accents range from mid-century modern light fixtures to antlers arranged as wall sculpture.

"Everything is rustic, but playful and happy," Brian says. The most emphatic nod to cabin style comes in the master bedroom, where an upholstered plaid headboard wall and a deep green and navy palette create a preppy-meets-mountain effect.

For Brian, who splits his time between Atlanta and L.A., the home has become much more than the weekend retreat he'd envisioned. "This was going to be the place that I escaped to two times a month," he says, "And then I started to find myself so much more relaxed here than in the city. Unexpectedly, this has become kind of my primary residence."

A desk beneath the stairwell creates both a focal point and a functional workstation. The custom powder-coated steel railing, which replaced an old pine banister, ratchets up the visual drama.

One of Brian's first priorities in renovating the cabin was to replace small windows with larger versions that pull in ample light. In the living room, new French doors lead to the porch and blur the transition between indoors and out. Brian also cloaked the old fireplace in tile and added a recessed TV.

A marble-topped
steel table anchors
the dining area off
the kitchen. The
sisal rug that warms
the floor adds a
welcome layer
of rich texture to
the décor.

Previous Overleaf: White subway tile, in a herringbone pattern instead of the expect horizontal stacking, dresses the kitchen walls. Buffalo-check curtains and butcher-block countertops contrast with the modern cabinetry and fixtures.

∧ Brian designed the basement-level bunk room with his nephews in mind. Because it's so low, the view is mostly sky, so he chose rich, masculine navy paint as a complement. The painting above the sofa is the only piece of art bought specifically for the house—the others came from Brian's collection.

❯ Slim brass ladders provide access to the bunks without eating up floor space. Antler accents and traditional fabric patterns take the blue in a mountainous, rather than nautical, direction.

‹ Muted pea-green paint pulls in the colors of the foliage just outside this guest bedroom, which features spectacular views from the bed. Resin antlers and a collection of hats on the wall add a bit of homey flavor.

∧ Pine paneling in the bathroom got coat upon coat of white paint to freshen it without erasing its rustic undertones. A new shower supplanted an old tub. Upholstered doors with brass nailhead trim repeat the deep, woodsy green of the shower curtain.

Dream Home Come True

Sturdy but stylish furnishings transform the renovated porch into a haven for alfresco meals, casual gatherings and relaxation. Brass accents, such as the chandelier, echo those throughout the house and elevate the space beyond a typical outdoor room.

GROWING
NEW ROOTS

—— CASHIERS, NORTH CAROLINA ——

To call this mountain retreat a spec house doesn't do it justice. Although architect Stan Dixon may not have had a client's wish list in hand, he devoted every bit as much care and consideration to the details as he does for his bespoke homes. The difference? "I was able to create my own storyline," says Stan, who owns the Atlanta firm D. Stanley Dixon Architect, Inc. "I wanted to do a mountain house that removed itself from some of the stereotypical clichés that people sometimes use in the mountains."

As his plans began to take shape, the spectacular views and woodland surroundings dictated the home's design. "The setting really called for this house to be rambling and asymmetrical," Stan says. The linchpin is a center section with a veneer of hand-hewn reclaimed timbers, anchored with mortar, in keeping with the traditional construction method of a log home. Stone and clapboard wings spread outward from either side.

"It's designed to emulate a log cabin that has been added onto over time," Stan says. "The log portion of the house is very symmetrical and very balanced, which gives it focus."

A controlled mix of materials keeps the look cohesive. "When you do a house that has more than one exterior material, it can get pretty tricky and look too gimmicky," Stan says. "It was important to me to continue to edit. The windows are the elements that really tie

‹ Architect Stan Dixon artfully blended a mixture of traditional materials to create the impression of a home that had evolved over the years. Elements such as the double-hung windows keep it in step with the architectural vernacular in the Cashiers area.

˥ The strong symmetry of the log portion of the home is reinforced by small details, such as twin lanterns beside the entry door and oversize planters on the porch.

› Stan and his team added a timber in the corner where the log façade meets the stone one, in order to make the junction seamless. A consistent color palette between the logs, stone and chinking underscores the visual harmony.

Growing New Roots

the house together; they're all very consistent and relate from one space of the house to the next."

The same harmonious blend of styles carries through to the interior. Instead of logs, however, the walls of the home's core feature horizontal wood paneling, which prevents the house from feeling dark. Stan explains, "We mixed the lighter, brighter painted surface with the timber framing of the logs to create the story."

For the shallow entrance hall that transverses the front of the house, Stan purposefully kept the entry ceiling low—just seven and a half feet tall—to evoke a cabin feel. Exposed framing overhead combines with reclaimed, hand-hewn beams and posts for the illusion of a timber-frame home. Take a few steps in, however, and one of the most dramatic contrasts bursts into view: the ceiling of the central living and dining area soars to 18 feet. That visual push-pull is part of what makes the layout so arresting. While the living/dining space is the most expansive, it's offset by smaller rooms that keep the house from feeling cavernous. The stepped-down library, for instance, is capped by a barn wood ceiling and warmed by golden yellow walls, which meld into a cozy envelope. Even the porch has tieback draperies that foster an air of enclosure.

A mixture of antique and updated elements throughout the interior aptly straddles the line be-

tween past and present. Tobacco sticks from North Carolina, once used to dry tobacco leaves, got new life as a living room balcony railing. Pocket doors that can be pulled to enclose the kitchen include restoration-glass panes. In the kitchen, a single

⌃ A high wainscoting wraps around the walls of the back entry. Shaker-style wooden pegs add to its aesthetic as well as its function—providing a place to hang purses, jackets, leashes, fishing equipment and more.

› In the entry, an old kilim rug adds color and a tribal motif. Designer Kathleen Rivers paired it with antique Chinese consoles for a blend of cultural influences.

reclaimed beam embedded above a recessed cook-top niche represents a fresh take on an old-fashioned hearth.

Kathleen Rivers, of Kathleen Rivers Interior Design, orchestrated the decor. She took much the same approach to the furnishings and finishes as Stan did to the architecture, playing honed against sleek and vintage against modern. Rich, subdued neutrals and restrained patterns enhance the colors and textures of the wood and stone.

In collaborating with Stan, Kathleen says, she grew to love the layout so much that she considered purchasing the house for herself. "To me, it is simply one of the most perfect floor plans ever envisioned," she says. "The living/dining/kitchen and outdoor spaces

Stan left the architectural framework of the balcony overlooking the living room exposed; thus, the framework becomes part of the décor. A large-scale modern painting by Sally Benedict, over the mantel, adds a fresh undertone to the traditional furnishings.

flow effortlessly from one to another. The library is private yet accessible, as is the master bedroom. It's truly one of the most charming and livable houses I have ever had the privilege of working on."

The scheme supports Stan's vision of cabin-style coziness couched within modern square footage. "It's sizable," Stan says of the house, "but it doesn't feel huge and overwhelming. It feels warm and comfortable." Put simply: It's a big home with an even bigger heart.

〈 Pots and pans stored on open shelves beneath the cooktop echo the log-cabin tradition of storing cookware on the fireplace hearth. The cooktop area is finished with rusticated stucco for visual texture.

〉 Stan designed the kitchen island in the style of a gateleg table, which features drop-down leaves on either end and turned legs. The ochre finish enlivens an otherwise subdued space.

Overleaf: The architecture in the library has an Early American feel, in keeping with the backstory of the cabin having been enlarged over time. Rich mustard walls appear luminous against earthy brown accents. A textured sisal carpet grounds the space.

Growing New Roots

< On the porch, hemlock log posts and railings blend in with the trees and the view beyond, keeping the focus on the beauty of the natural setting. Draperies soften the architecture of the porch and can be pulled shut for coziness or to screen out bad weather.

∧ Soft neutrals allow the home's lush, wooded setting to take center stage. Locally made Cashiers furniture blends easily with antiques and flea market finds.

Growing New Roots

A HASTY RETREAT

—— CASHIERS, NORTH CAROLINA ——

Interior designer Kathleen Rivers isn't one to back down from a challenge. Her clients Kreis and Sandy Beall, then owners of the luxury retreat Blackberry Farm in Tennessee, had bought a lot at the Chattooga Club in Cashiers, with the intent of building a mountain cabin. Sandy set a deadline for Kathleen and local builder Dearl Stewart to have the entire project done within just nine months. With work to begin in September, he wanted to move in by Memorial Day of the following year.

With such a compact schedule, Sandy "left us to make decisions to keep things moving at Mach speed," Kathleen says. With the architectural plans still taking shape, Dearl and Sandy sourced salvaged logs from dismantled cabins in Kentucky and Tennessee and had them shipped to Cashiers. Dearl's amazing team of local carpenters went at the project passionately. Doorways, windows and other structural elements took shape on the fly, as the puzzle pieces of logs arrived and dictated the flow of the home.

Immersing herself in the project and with her assistant Elizabeth Newman coordinating details, Kathleen loved the twin challenges of the deadline and creating interiors for such a complex space. Kreis, a brilliant designer in her own right, gave Kathleen the reins on the design work. They both loved the earth tones so prevalent in the mountains, colors that would complement the walls and reflect and enhance the rich greens and browns of the landscape "Nothing could be more intoxicating than for one extremely talented designer to tell another to take the ball and run, and that is exactly what happened," says Kathleen.

Neither Kathleen nor Kreis thought the decor should feel as rustic as the log backdrop. "The design aesthetic was meant to feel comfortable and lodge-like, but not primitive. The interior was designed not to be of the period, but instead to look and feel country cosmopolitan," says Kathleen.

Although the Bealls embraced the idea of calling the cabin The Abe, as a tribute to Abraham Lincoln's log-cabin roots, Lincoln would have had a tough time getting his head around the home's luxurious fabrics and fine antiques. The furnishings represent a virtual Grand Tour of Europe: an oversize screen from Lisbon; an old factory sewing table from Belgium; an English-inspired living area at the heart of the home.

Perhaps no space in the house showcases the arresting contrasts in texture, pedigree and period as fully as the main living space: an open, rambling room that functions as dining room, bar, lounge and more. "The scale of the main room was daunting. However, by creating multiple seating areas and

⌐ Builder Dearl Stewart improvised these exterior balconies as part of the home's design.

❯ The rustic wooden gate and the home's gardens were designed by Atlanta landscape architect Mary Palmer Dargan.

this

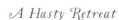

A Hasty Retreat

stacking paintings tall on the wall, we were able to create an inviting space full of warmth and comfort," Kathleen says. Her extensive trips to England and France, touring grand country homes, provided much of the inspiration for the eclectic layering of textures, rugs and art, all of which add to the familiar yet unexpected charm of the house.

The cabin has since changed ownership, and its current owners, the Cay family of Savannah and Charleston, have lent their own taste and style by adding personal touches. Even so, Kathleen says, "it continues to be a welcoming haven for families and friends of all ages, with its soft surroundings to provide a retreat from the heat of southern summers, or in winter, to offer warm gatherings by the fire."

‹ An arrangement of disparate finds in the entry hall—croquet mallets, fishing creel, antlers and 19th-century North Carolina pottery—all speak to the local lifestyle.

› This floral embroidered chair creates a dainty counterpoint to the brawny log walls.

A Hasty Retreat

∧ An antique wooden hutch, thought to be from Tennessee, is flanked by a pair of 19th-century English dog portraits. Kathleen added a collection of Southern baskets and pottery on top.

≫ A screen found in Lisbon hangs above an antique sewing table from Belgium. The owners gave their permission for Kathleen to purchase it sight unseen, trusting that if she liked it, they would too. The long table doubles as a bar for gatherings.

Although the kitchen is new, the cabinets were crafted to mimic an antique hutch that was integrated into the space.

‹ Kathleen designed the white bedroom in homage to one she had seen and loved years ago. "Absolutely nothing is softer and prettier than all white against a complex backdrop," Rivers says.

Antique oval needlepoint pieces in the bedroom are surrounded by wood frames, custom-designed by Cashiers artisan Chad Collins. He also crafted the bathroom mirror.

A Hasty Retreat

< A whimsical moss-covered bench highlights the cabin's rustic outdoor pergola.

> On the porch, wicker furniture and tole-bucket lamps mingle with a patchwork contemporary Moroccan rug found at an antique market and a mantel that Stewart designed in collaboration with a stoneworker.

HISTORY *at* HEART

—— McCALLA, ALABAMA ——

The best things are worth the wait. Just ask Walter Russell, who for years had wanted an old log cabin for his 200-acre farm west of Birmingham. After a drawn-out search, he connected with an Alabama furniture maker and log cabin expert named Butch Fuller, who'd recently secured a story-and-a-half cabin in Woodbury, Kentucky. When Walter, who owns American Lumber, came up to take a look at it, he was sold right away.

The cabin, built in 1812 and enlarged in 1825, was a treasure for its ingenious detailing and workmanship as well as its history. "It would have been a grand home for its time," Butch says. "It is magnificent." But no one had lived there in forty years and time had taken its toll. Dried tobacco stalks and open windows with ladders spoke to its use as crop storage and a hunting blind, respectively. Inside, the logs had been plastered with newspaper, cheaper than new chinking. One entire wall was rotted out; the roofing had deteriorated along with it. Still, most of the massive poplar logs were in surprisingly good shape, considering how little upkeep they'd had. And the hand-cut, herringbone-pattern sandstone fireplace was intact, though missing its oval keystone (eventually discovered under a pile of debris).

Over a late-summer weekend, Walter, Butch and a small crew started the tedious task of numbering the logs, taking them down one by one and loading them up for the move. They were in up to their elbows when a car rumbled down the dirt road. Out hopped an

‹ Walter added a wraparound screened-in porch to the cabin, which provides not only outdoor living space but also a measure of protection for the logs. The self-locking half dovetail system, so effective that the original cabin construction needed no nails or pegs, is clearly visible at the corner.

∧ The cabin's old stoop stone has a place of honor, tucked alongside the lower-level foundation.

elderly gentleman, none too pleased at seeing the cabin dismantled. "It turned out this guy was 85 years old," Butch says. "And he said, 'I was born in this cabin.'"

By the man's account, he and his wife had driven up from South Carolina on a hunch that he needed to visit the "home place," which had first belonged to his great-great-grandfather. As he reminisced, "I didn't know if I could believe him or not, but after a while it started making sense to me," Walter says. "So I told him, 'You're welcome to come down after I get it reassembled. You can stay as long as you want to.'" True to his word, when the cabin was finished the following year, Walter arranged for the couple to fly down and stay in it as the very first guests.

He and Butch took pains to match the new materials as closely as possible to the originals.

History at Heart

< A porch swing on the lower level offers a spot for Walter to enjoy the views over his property. He kept the landscaping simple, taking care not to plant shrubbery or other foliage close to the logs in order to guard against rot.

⌐ The cabin's original owner, Thomas Douglas Wand, carved his initials into an exterior log.

∧ A doll's shoe and a signed piece of chinking were two of the small treasures found as the crew dismantled the cabin for the move to Alabama.

"I didn't want to cut any corners," Walter says. Hand-hewn logs replaced the rotted wall, and Walter chose wooden roof shakes appropriate to the period. A local blacksmith forged all of the hardware; the windowpanes came from a Birmingham company that specializes in restoration glass. Although the chinking is a modern rubberized material that can absorb the cabin's slight movement as it settles, it looks identical to the old-fashioned type.

Clues along the process offered a window into the cabin's past. During demolition, the crew found a piece of chinking signed by an A. B. Scott, who, they later learned, had been a close friend and neighbor of the original owners. A broken doll's shoe unearthed from the walls signaled the Germanic tradition of hiding a baby's shoe in the chinking for good luck. "Over and over again, we had little moments that we didn't expect," Butch says.

But the most rewarding discovery was still to come. The cabin had been completed for six months before Walter noticed a detail he'd missed. "One day when I was showing it to some friends, I saw this shadow on one of the old logs," he says. "It was so worn that you could barely see it. It had three initials on it: TDW."

Walter rushed inside to pull out a sheet of paperwork that the old gentleman had given him when he visited. Sure enough, the original owner's name was listed as Thomas Douglas Wand.

"To be able to put that together from that guy coming down there that weekend, . . . it was just meant for me to have this cabin."

< One of Walter's priorities was to restore the fireplace, which had been converted to a wood stove. The old-fashioned cooking crane was made by Alabama blacksmith Neil Faulkenberry.

∧ Adze and broadaxe marks are visible along the logs. A narrow ledger rail on the wall supports the floor joists.

∧ Hanging pegs were preserved from the original cabin.

Cabin expert and
furniture maker
Butch Fuller
crafted the chairs
and other pieces
for the house. A
ladder leads to the
sleeping loft. The
floor joists and
also the ledger
rail have a bead
design, done with
a small tool called
a scratch stock.

History at Heart

A HOME *in* THREE ACTS

—— RAPPAHANNOCK COUNTY, VIRGINIA ——

Joe Svatos still marvels at how close he came to tearing down a piece of American history. He'd just bought a 200-acre property in rural Rappahannock County, Virginia, seduced by the gorgeous riverfront setting and Blue Ridge Mountain views. There was only one eyesore: a dilapidated building tucked on a mountainside, abandoned and left to decay.

Although Joe, a Washington, D.C.–based developer, assumed the structure was left over from the resettlement of residents due to the creation of nearby Shenandoah National Park, instinct told him to have a salvage expert evaluate it, just in case. The expert pried off a bit of the worn red siding, and he and Joe glimpsed a tantalizing surprise: a strip of chinking sandwiched between hand-hewn double dovetailed logs. Later, the salvage expert would date the house to the 1790s. But Joe already knew that he had a treasure on his hands. And there was a bonus: as the siding was stripped further, it revealed an 1850s balloon-frame addition, connected to the cabin by an original stone chimney in solid condition.

"At that point, I thought, 'I need to at least stabilize these buildings so they don't rot and fall down,'" Joe says. "That was the start of the process that led to creating this retreat."

In passing, Joe's salvage expert mentioned an 1840s chestnut cabin slated for demolition in Howard County, Maryland. It was the missing puzzle piece, Joe realized, that

would turn this visual odd couple into a cohesive unit, a mountain getaway where he could shrug off the pressures of city life. Now all he needed was the right architect to bring it to life.

Joe tapped architect David Haresign of the Washington, DC, firm Bonstra Haresign, whom Joe had gotten to know professionally over the years. David, who specializes in contemporary commercial design, wasn't at all sure the project was for him. But when he rode out to the site, he was captivated. "From the cabin itself you can see Old Rag Mountain, an iconic mountain on the Appalachian Trail. I used to hike that as a boy."

Joe was adamant that the home needed to work for modern-day living; he didn't want to "have it as a museum," he says. Still, "we absolutely had to respect the history. Whatever contemporary insertions we put in here couldn't be out of line in terms of texture or feel."

The original 1790s cabin, slated to become the main living area and library, had a $7^1/_2$-foot ceiling that both Joe and David agreed needed to come out. "It would have been dark, and I would have been bumping my head on the beams," Joe says. Removing that element opened up a story and a half of clear space that he likens to a cathedral or a sanctuary. In the Howard County cabin, the team eliminated better than half of the second floor, crafting a steel-beam loft bedroom with a complete kitchen below.

‹ The cabin imported from Howard County, Maryland, was not as tall as it needed to be for the way owner Joe Svatos envisioned its function. A log cabin professional sourced an antique chestnut barn of the same vintage to provide enough logs to increase the cabin's height.

⌃ The connection between the balloon-frame addition and Howard County cabin creates a sense of visual lightness and transparency.

A Home in Three Acts

《 Although architect David Haresign preserved the original door and window openings on the public-facing side of the cabin, he added large expanses of windows on the other side so that Joe could enjoy the river and mountain views.

∧ The frame of the barn, which serves for both entertaining and storage, was originally a corncrib from southern Pennsylvania. David reused the frames but modified the building with larger openings for smoother flow.

〈 Joe and David collaborated on plans for a curvilinear stone wall with a cairn at one edge. The mason fit each stone in carefully to create its cohesive design. "Instead of a traditional rubble wall, it's really a work of art," Joe says.

A Home in Three Acts

^ Most of the second floor in the Howard County cabin was removed to create the sense of volume that Joe wanted. To stabilize the walls, David installed a system of horizontal steel plates and vertical dowels concealed within the wood and chinking.

> The new steel-beam loft includes horizontal railings that respect the orientation of the log walls.

Although David and Joe inserted contemporary materials where appropriate, such as the glass floor that connects the nineteenth-century house and the chestnut cabin, they took pains to do so in ways that would enhance the rustic roots. Any area clad in new wood, such as the kitchen island, has a markedly different style to lend visual separation. "If it's in the building that has logs, the woods run vertically so there's no confusion," David explains.

Paradoxically, high-tech systems help to preserve the home's integrity. Hydronic radiant floors provide heat; air-conditioning flows vertically from the crawl space below the house. A new basement added beneath the Howard County cabin conceals what David terms "the mechanical guts and brains of the building."

Joe deliberately kept the decor pared down so as not to detract from the beauty of the logs. "It's almost Shaker-like," he says. "A lot of the furniture is contemporary, but simple." Although he incorporated a few period-appropriate antiques, the home's modern elements make them appear fresh.

The real star of this retreat remains its natural surroundings. "As soon as you get here, as soon as you arrive, you feel a peace," Joe says. "Land and landscapes and settings—they're not all created equal. I have not been on another property in this part of Virginia that has this combination of driveway by the river, view of the mountains, and big trees. It's really a spiritual setting."

≪ Joe and David designed streamlined Windsor-style chairs for the dining room and had a local woodworker craft them. A cabinetmaker fashioned the custom table.

∧ Joe was adamant that he wanted to use pale green paint on the kitchen cabinetry for a punch of color. The gentle hue brings in a bit of the outdoors and breaks up the concentrated wood tones.

‹ Simple granite countertops recede against the hefty log architecture and eye-catching cabinet color.

A Home in Three Acts

The original log
cabin on the
property and the
balloon-frame
addition share a
dual-sided fireplace
with a common
chimney (also seen
on page 112).

The glass-floor
walkway is one
of the few overtly
contemporary
elements in the
home yet doesn't
detract from its
historic integrity.
The desk and chair
are pre–Civil War
antiques.

∧ Joe kept the décor as simple as possible and hung very little art so as not to draw attention away from the logs. The headboard of the bed doubles as a closet on the back side.

‹ Hardware hand-forged locally helps to maintain the home's sense of period and place.

› Although the steel that forms the loft feels rustic in its own way, it also adds a contemporary reference that Joe enjoys.

HUNTING DOWN HISTORY

— COLUMBUS, GEORGIA —

Rick Spitzmiller has always held a passion for historic preservation. Before launching his career as one of Atlanta's premier residential architects, he served as architectural advisor for the Historic Savannah Foundation in coastal Georgia. So when longtime friend and client Dan Amos called to ask for his help restoring an old log cabin, Rick jumped at the chance to unleash his inner history buff.

"By and large, when people these days build log houses, they seem to do a lot of kit building," says Rick, cofounder of the firm Spitzmiller and Norris. "That's a totally different animal from finding a marvelous indigenous building and giving it a new lease on life."

The 1830s cabin, built top to bottom from heart pine in rural Tennessee, had been slated for demolition before Dan got wind of it. In search of a lodge for hunt breakfasts and fishing excursions on his farm in Columbus, Georgia, he stepped in and scooped up the little structure. "It held great appeal to him that he would be preserving a building that otherwise was going to be lost," says Rick.

The cabin now rests amid a stand of trees near the edge of a lake, looking for all the world like it grew there. Rick, who owns a historic home of the same period as the cabin, understood the importance of modifying and modernizing it in a way that wouldn't erode its integrity. "If what drew Dan to it was its historicism and its quality of construction and the materials that really have made it what it is, it would have been foolish to ruin those by doing insensitive renovations or additions," Rick says. "We tried to be very careful to insert new components as appreciatively as we could."

Chief among those components: an open-loft bedroom in the original attic space, straight across from an expansive glass window wall created to showcase the lake view. "That didn't rob the building of any of its period grace," Rick says. "When you're upstairs, you can lie in bed and watch the ducks swimming by."

He also expanded the entry doors to smooth the transition for large groups of people passing through during hunting getaways. Cedar roof shingles and a dry-stacked stone foundation and fireplace are true to the cabin's era. Where new wood elements had to be added, such as the kitchen flooring and the staircase that leads to the loft, the team chose either white pine or reclaimed heart pine, in keeping with the original structure. It was brought into the twenty-first century while asserting its historical pedigree.

Because the cabin was to be a hub for entertaining, Rick also added a kitchen and a small bathroom onto the back. While neither room pretends to be primitive, their clean design and lack of ornamentation blend fluidly with the home's original core. Both repeat the cabin's woodsy brown and creamy white palette, dotted throughout with dabs of red. Antique furniture—and not too much of it—keeps company with tailored, masculine seating and a handful of unpretentious accents.

Both the historian and the architect in Rick still marvel at having revived such a remarkable piece of the rural southern past. Knowing that Dan could have built anything he wanted on the site makes it even sweeter.

⌐ On the new window wall overlooking the lake, deep gray-green paint keeps the addition unprepossessing. Cedar roof shingles are appropriate to the cabin's period.

> Notched corners fit together in an interlocking pattern that strengthens the cabin's construction. The logs are eased so that rainwater runs off rather than pooling.

>> Rot-resistant locust tree trunks act as columns for the front porch.

∧ A custom bench bears the name of Dan Amos's property, Soma Farms (his last name spelled backward).

˥ The lake is a natural habitat for ducks and other fowl. Watching them is a relaxing pastime.

› The cabin is positioned to take full advantage of the beautiful lake views.

Hunting Down History

≪ New casement windows let in air and light without detracting from the cabin's bones. A simple wooden mantel tops the dry-stacked stone fireplace.

‹ Heart-pine flooring and white-painted pine walls combine with the log walls to form an envelope that is sensitive to the original construction. Dan and his wife are avid antiquers and sourced many furnishings and accents appropriate to the cabin's era.

Hunting Down History

< The interaction between old and new is clear in the main living area. Because the ceiling of the original cabin is quite low, architect Rick Spitzmiller offset that with a clerestory-style area along the fireplace wall.

∧ The kitchen cabinetry was crafted from roughly planed white-pine boards. An upper shelf holds cookware in a nod to the rudimentary storage of 19th-century kitchens.

⌐ Batten doors and period hardware enhance the aged feel. The beams that form the ceiling of the main room are notched crosswise into the uppermost timber.

Hunting Down History

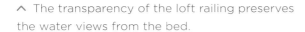 The transparency of the loft railing preserves the water views from the bed.

> A simple white pedestal sink saves floor space in the small downstairs bath.

>> White walls, ceiling and bed linens combine to bounce light around the loft, an arresting contrast with the cozy, close feel of the living area.

Hunting Down History

LAID-BACK LUXURY

— CASHIERS, NORTH CAROLINA —

It all began with a simple plan to beat the heat. Invited for a summertime visit to the North Carolina mountains, Linda and Darwin James welcomed the chance to get away from the smothering temps at their Tulsa home. Although they'd toyed with the idea of buying a vacation retreat, they'd never given much thought to Cashiers. But that soon changed.

"The more we stayed in Cashiers, the more we liked it," says Linda, owner of Linda James Antiques. What sealed the deal, though, was a walk through the Cashiers Designer Show House. Friend and renowned designer Charles Faudree, who had helped with their home in Tulsa, had decorated a room in the house, which blended a 1790s log cabin with an 1830s one. The Jameses came to see his work, but they stayed for the home's graceful bones and gorgeous setting: 43 rolling acres, with a tree-ringed lake below and an old horse barn beyond.

"It's extremely serene, totally peaceful and private," Linda says. By the time they headed back west, the cabin bug had bitten them hard. Charles felt as strongly about the place as they did. They made an offer, and he later told Linda he'd prayed all night that they'd get it.

Keys in hand, the couple didn't hesitate to put their own stamp on the estate, previously christened Reflections. They fenced in 10 acres of pasture and built a new barn for their Tennessee Walking horses. The old barn became a man cave and fishing shack. Lavish landscaping, a redone front gate and other enhancements took an already spectacular setting over the top.

The renovations continued inside, where Linda and Darwin revamped the kitchen and bathrooms. They completely enclosed a dogtrot between the two original

Previous Overleaf: When Linda and Darwin purchased the home after its stint as the Cashiers Designer Show House, they bought a few of the furnishings that had been used, including this burlap-covered swing on the back porch. Two red chairs found locally round out the seating area, which has a great view of the lake.

⌐ The antique bench on back porch, outfitted with custom pillows, came from the Jameses' friend and designer Charles Faudree.

〉 A road sign out front bears the home's moniker.

〉〉 Guests driving in approach the rear façade first—a stunning tableau with the lake at the foot of the sloping lawn.

Laid-Back Luxury

cabins, adding new windows and climatization. Local builder Dearl Stewart, who had handled the previous owners' renovation and understood the home's quirks, spearheaded the overhaul. As Linda puts it, "He knew where all the skeletons were buried."

For the interior, Charles and Linda pulled the palette from the surroundings, weaving in lots of soft greens, deep golds and rich browns. Slightly at odds with Darwin over how a mountain home should be decorated—Linda is a little more formal than her husband—she and Charles compromised: chic antiques mixed with horn accents and antlers; fine rugs on the plank floors; majolica and transferware hung on the rough-hewn log walls.

For Linda, decorating the cabin became a welcome change of pace from her formal French home and her antiques shop in Tulsa. She embraced the chance to infuse a little local color. "People really love their Black Forest antiques here," she says. "That's not something I'd have in Oklahoma, but I do have a few pieces in this house."

While the Jameses spend the most time at the cabin in summer, each season carries its own rewards. Spring brings rhododendron blossoms; summer has boating on the lake; and fall offers a glorious display of foliage. Says Linda, simply, "It's just a special place."

∧ In the hallway outside the den, a country French shelf bears a black tole tray and equestrian hats, the latter a nod to the Jameses' love of horses.

> This wall, now home to an antique Black Forest china cabinet and bar, was originally a pass-through to the kitchen. To remodel it, builder Dearl Stewart managed the difficult task of finding logs to match the originals. The French loveseat is a favorite perch for the family dog to wait for people to walk in the door.

Previous Overleaf: A laurel-branch stair railing gives the living room a top note of rough-hewn charm. The fireplace is original to the cabin.

≪ Linda added a small table in the entry as an intimate spot to entertain small groups. Formal accents—a bull's-eye mirror with majolica, a tapestry hanging—balance the simple rush-seat chairs and trestle table.

∧ Charles designed corner cabinets specifically to fit the show house dining room, though he ultimately was given a different room to decorate for the event. Leather-and-plaid chairs surround a custom-made dining table.

< Shiny gold mirrors and blue-and-white English china dress up this dining room commode, painted white.

> Matching trumeau mirrors stand behind French commodes used as night tables in the master bedroom. The antique bench, found locally, was reupholstered in a tapestry fabric.

Overleaf: The Jameses enhanced the home's rear landscaping, adding rose beds and more along the pathway. They also built a new dock from which family and guests can fish in the trout-stocked lake.

∧ The wraparound open porch off the master bedroom is a favorite spot for the family to nestle down on cool evenings or catch the mountain breeze on warm ones. A new antler chandelier is a nod to classic mountain style.

⟩ At one corner of the porch, a delicate bamboo étagère and French chair bring a little refinement to the rough log walls.

Laid-Back Luxury

MIX, MASTERED

—— LAKE HARTWELL, GEORGIA ——

There's going outside your comfort zone, and then there's leaving your comfort zone in the dust. Athens, Georgia, designer Laura Stearns, known for her modern, urban aesthetic, had never tackled a project quite like the one that her client Dave Mulkey had given her: a retreat on 45 lakeside acres, comprised of two small guest cottages and a bunkhouse. With four children, Dave wanted it to evoke his childhood, during which his family had spent summers at their rustic woodland cabin in Griffin, Georgia.

"I was really longing for a retreat where we could replicate those experiences for the kids," Dave says.

Dave wanted the cabins to feel as though they had evolved over time. Rick Spitzmiller and Robert Norris, of Atlanta residential design firm Spitzmiller & Norris, handled the architectural plans. Rather than staying within period confines, the team decided to use traditional cabin elements as a springboard that would inform the design in spirit.

"The buildings were all planned with the idea of using materials that were indigenous to the property: fieldstone for the foundation walls and chimneys; hewn logs with chinking for the exterior siding; heart pine flooring for the interiors along with washed and painted wood walls and ceilings," says Rick.

∧ A portal at the center of the bunkhouse allows the eye to travel through to the lake beyond.

❯ New timbers were cut, stained and layered with plaster chinking to evoke the impression of a traditional log cabin. The fieldstone foundation calls to mind the rock pilings on which such cabins often sat.

Tongue-and-groove and shiplap paneling take the place of ordinary drywall; hand-forged hardware adds to the layers of texture and heft that Dave wanted. "When I grab a doorknob, I want it to feel like a heavy, wrought, forged doorknob," he says.

True to her style, Laura shook up the design with a little edginess. A twig ceiling caps the kitchen; a powder room sink pedestal is crafted from a thick tree stump. In a dining area, another stump from the same tree, topped with a free-form slab of wood, stands in for a traditional table. Laura collaborated on those elements with local wood artisan Pat Quinn, who did all the cabinetry in the house from materials sourced on site.

A concrete trough sink spans one wall in the kids' bunkhouse bathroom—not unlike an old-fashioned summer camp, if camp bathrooms had bespoke cabinetry and stacks of lush linens. In

Mix, Mastered

the bunkhouse, a dozen recessed sleeping niches are framed with curtains that pull shut. Dave likens the structure to a fort, where kids can have privacy yet be close to the other cabins on-site.

Honed finishes and imperfections keep surfaces and fixtures from becoming too sleek to blend in well. "Each element has its own patina," Laura says. She chose natural textiles such as leather and linen—period appropriate, yet given an updated spin.

What Dave loves most is the way the property has grown organically over time. Before the cabins took shape, the family camped on the land, enjoying the idyllic setting that reminds Dave so much of his early years. They still make a point of savoring simple pleasures: a fire ring by the lake where they can roast s'mores; hay wagon rides; fireworks in the meadow.

"We've created all these little things that burn memories into kids' minds," Dave says.

Because each of the cabins on the property is relatively compact, the design team saved space via built-ins, such as these shelves in the living area. Deep neutrals and sturdy fabrics lend a decidedly masculine air. Recessed window-seat niches extend the usable space and provide a vantage point from which to enjoy the views.

Mix, Mastered

∧ Wood artisan Pat Quinn custom-crafted Dutch doors for the cabins. Ancient Oushak rugs are elegant but not too precious for a lakeside home.

∧ To give the kitchen cabinets a weathered feel, Laura chose two wall paint colors used elsewhere in the house and had them layered on, then rubbed in spots. The island is an antique butcher-block table that has seen plenty of use over the years.

The live-edge kitchen table was made from a piece of wood indigenous to the property.

Mix, Mastered

∧ The tree-stump powder room vanity, which slips into a corner, makes smart use of a small space.

˥ This bath deftly mixes old-fashioned and modern. Traditional woods and honed stone flooring mingle with a minimalist sink and faucet.

〉 Paneling turned on the diagonal, rather than running straight across, adds a little dynamism to an otherwise quiet backdrop. A few dark notes help to ground the light palette.

< Each of the bunks in the kids' bunkhouse includes recessed shelving for books and small treasures.

^ The bathroom is well organized with multiple sinks and under-counter storage to accommodate a full bunk room of children.

∧ The homeowner wanted a magical spot on the property for the children to claim as their own. Contractor Curtis Whitsel incorporated his wish list—a rope swing, pirate net and more—into a custom-built treehouse tucked between three white oak trees.

❮ This porch railing represents a rough-hewn take on classic Chippendale design.

❯ Laura had hanging twig daybeds and other complementary furnishings crafted for the screened-in porch.

OLD CABIN, NEW TRICKS

— HIGHLANDS, NORTH CAROLINA —

If Carole Weaks has one piece of advice for decorating a mountain cabin, it's this: Don't overthink it. "It's something you have to figure out by trial and error—what is going to settle in and feel right with everything else naturally going on in the environment," says Carole, owner of C. Weaks Interiors in Atlanta.

Her theory rings throughout this 1928 North Carolina home, an original by renowned local craftsman Joe Webb and one of the oldest cabins in Highlands Country Club. Relying on instinct rather than rigid rules, and eye-appeal rather than pedigree, she helped the owners create a retreat that's anything but typical, yet feels perfectly at home in its surroundings.

A first glimpse of the exterior signals the surprises that await. The pine and chestnut logs got a coat of pale gray paint for a clean, cottage-like effect. Left natural on the inside, they frame the home's showpiece: a gangly, twisting rhododendron stair rail, a signature Joe Webb touch. The rail is as much visual sculpture as functional construction, and its free-form beauty anchors the cabin firmly in its natural roots.

Despite the charm of the wood, "the house was fairly dark," Carole says. "These particular clients really liked color and warmth. They wanted it cozy and a little less rustic."

Nowhere is that more evident than in the dining room—Carole's biggest decorating challenge. Small and narrow, with a very low ceiling, it required a little ingenuity to furnish. The solution: a banquette at one end, with the table and chairs clustered around it. A more conventional layout would have left room for little else.

At first blush, the palette feels softer than a cabin's sturdy bones might dictate. But look closer, and its strength comes forward. Reds and dusty greens give heft to the crisp patterns and solid neutrals. Common threads tie in with the architecture: warm melons and ruddy browns that echo the logs; creams and putty grays that pick up the chinking. The colors are very American, with a subtle, sophisticated spin.

Given the rugged backdrop, some designers might have gone for robust, country-flavored furnishings. Carole took the opposite approach, deftly mixing her clients' collection of elegant antiques with traditional upholstered seating and refined, leggy tables. Modern artwork keeps company with vintage jugs and formal lamps.

Oddly, the disparate furnishings give the cabin a stronger sense of authenticity than rooms full of period pieces. The result: a home that remains loyal to its roots, yet feels unique and completely personal.

Soft gray paint on the cabin's exterior logs gives this cabin an updated spin without obscuring its roots or making it look too modern. The neutral color also allows the surrounding natural foliage—bright green in summer, brilliant jewel tones in fall—to take the spotlight.

Old Cabin, New Tricks

< The free-form rhododendron stair railing by Joe Webb, the home's craftsman, is a signature in many of his cabins. A trestle table anchors the living area and adds a rustic element that relates to the log architecture.

^ A hand-hooked rag rug adds just enough soft color to give the living area personality. The antique tole planter on the table picks up the reds in the pillow fabrics.

^ This odd-size niche beneath the stairs presented a design challenge. A console table from the homeowners' collection fit perfectly and put to work what would have been wasted space.

Old Cabin, New Tricks

∧ A vintage painted cart got new life as a side table.

⌐ Designer Carole Weaks found this whimsical card table and chairs in France.

> Although the dining room has a limited palette, warm blues and rich melons, layers of texture and pattern make it feel vibrant. The colors play off the mellowness of the wood.

< Two red-and-cream fabrics add a youthful, happy mien to this twin bedroom, used for the owners' grandchildren.

^ A dark wooden headboard with a rattan insert stands out crisply against the pale green grass cloth wallpaper in this bedroom.

Old Cabin, New Tricks

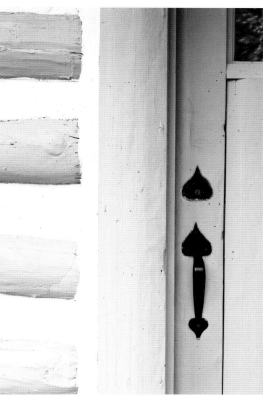

On the porch, a sloped wood-beam ceiling fosters a sense of coziness and ties in with the colors of the furniture. Just off the living and dining area, the porch helps to smooth out circulation when the owners entertain.

Old Cabin, New Tricks

A STORIED PAST

—— LAKE TOXAWAY, NORTH CAROLINA ——

When Atlantans Kay and Doug Ivester began the hunt for a guesthouse to include as part of their Lake Toxaway, North Carolina, vacation home, they couldn't find a suitable old cabin with a long and detailed history. So they did the next best thing: they built a new one and invented a backstory on their own.

"The story was about a dairy farmer who had moved to the Lake Toxaway area from Pennsylvania," Doug says. "He was there to supply milk and butter to the Lake Toxaway Inn, and in doing so he had a stone barn and a log cabin."

The Ivesters called upon architect Al Platt of Platt Architecture to help them bring this imaginary tale to life. Seeking to infuse as much authenticity as possible, they selected builder Bob Dylewski, known not just for his construction prowess but also for his expertise in sourcing antique woods. He has a passion for period architecture and furniture.

"Doug wanted to use indigenous American woods of this area. We didn't bring in exotic woods from different parts of the country or world," says Bob, "because it didn't fit the story or his taste."

Bob and his team combed the area for old cabins from which he could salvage logs and reuse them. Although the cabin was built with conventional exterior walls to make room for modern plumbing and wiring, the salvaged logs were split in half, then applied veneer-style and chinked both inside and out. "You cannot tell that it's not an original log cabin," Bob says.

Other vintage woods complement the log walls. Reclaimed local barn wood, custom milled and finished, cloaks other interior surfaces. The cabinetry in the house is reclaimed oak; the floors are heart pine, cut down from old ceiling beams. Atlanta designer Sherri Austin orchestrated the interiors, layering in lots of warm, rich reds, unadorned antiques and Americana-inspired accents.

The interior of the guest house is intentionally simple. Even so, unique touches—such as a timber-slab bathroom vanity—give it a singular character. "Doug was really open to brainstorming," Bob says. "He'd say, 'Have you ever done this before?' And we'd say no. And he'd say 'Good.'"

Doug is especially proud of Kay's ingenuity in outfitting the tiny kitchen. In the home's fictional narrative, "the original log cabin probably didn't have much of a kitchen in it," Doug says. "At some point the kitchen was added, probably in the early

‹ The porch was designed and equipped for frequent use; it's a favorite spot for the Ivesters to sip early morning coffee and watch the sunrise.

∧ The stonemasons who worked on the house took extreme care in placing each stone, with no detail overlooked.

∧ Although the pump house, complete with working hand pump, is newly built, it was designed to look as though it was original to the property.

❯ Because the team took such care to avoid modern materials, details such as air vents were constructed in a fashion true to the late 1800s.

❯❯ As part of the story that Doug and Kay wove for the cabin, they situated it next to the waterfall, imagining that the original owner would have wanted water accessible for the dairy cattle.

1900s." Kay found retro-style appliances to add the right dose of period flair. Details such as a punched-tin cabinet panel and an apron-front sink reinforce the vintage feel.

The Ivesters' house, Bob says, strikes an ideal balance of modern comfort couched within historically appropriate character. "People will want to do something rustic, but a lot of times what happens is that they take those materials and come up with a design that makes no sense with the era," he says. "The design of this home, in my opinion, speaks of a cabin that could have been built 150 or 200 years ago."

Doug puts it succinctly. "The message that a log cabin sends," he says, "is authenticity and respect for the past." Consider it a message heard loud and clear.

⌐ This rustic trellis was built to support Mandevilla vines in summer.

‹ Historically appropriate lighting from Bevolo Gas & Electric in New Orleans adds to the home's authenticity.

› The carriage house is home to a fully restored 1934 Ford Deluxe five-window coupe, just as the original owner in the Ivesters' story might have bought as his first car.

⌐ A stairwell leads to the loft bedroom, overlooking the sitting room with windows looking over the waterfall and lake.

∧ White-tail deer antlers compose a stunning chandelier in the stairwell.

‹ Most of the hardware, including that on this door, was hand-forged by a local artist; each piece is an individual work of art.

› An American flag art piece over the mantel represents the Ivesters' deep love of their country. Its red stripes are echoed in the room's upholstery and drapery fabrics.

‹ The antique-style range—outfitted with modern conveniences—sits at the heart of the kitchen that Kay designed.

ᐱ A small breakfast table and chairs creates a quiet spot for the couple to dine or relax.

ᐱ A reverse-punched tinwork panel, commissioned for the kitchen from a local artisan, adds eye-catching contrast to the cabinetry and evokes period flavor.

A Storied Past

« A plank vanity in
the bathroom is topped
with a copper bowl
retrofitted as a sink.

‹ The bedroom carries
out the palette of
warm reds sprinkled
throughout the cabin.
The brass bed is a family
heirloom.

A Storied Past

STRENGTH
of SPIRIT

Tom Hayes and Toby West have built their careers around fine design and antiques. So it stands to reason that when they talked about buying a second home in the mountains, they went straight for a classic: a 1920s log cabin built by Joe Webb.

"Neither Toby nor I would want a house up here with Sheetrock—we don't need a wine cellar and a theater," says Tom, who, along with Toby, owns Tom Hayes and Associates/ Toby West Ltd. "That is not what we're about."

When Tom and Toby bought the house in 1985, it had been well loved through the decades—though perhaps not in the exact way they might have preferred. Owners in the 1960s had added an awkward screened-in porch; others had propped the home on cinder blocks. All of them had left the bare-bones interior essentially untouched.

The charm and history eclipsed the downsides, however. Webb, who constructed dozens of log cabins in the area during the 1920s and '30s, was famous for doing it the old-fashioned way, without formal plans or machinery. Cabin enthusiasts consider the structures among Appalachia's crown jewels. Tom and Toby's house has the added distinction of being crafted completely from American chestnut, prolific in the area before a devastating blight in the first half of the twentieth century. As they laid plans to enlarge the 1,500-square-foot cabin to nearly 4,000 square feet, one of their biggest concerns was mitigating any brand-spanking-new feel that might undermine the historic roots. Local contractor Tommy Chambers, who handled the restoration and additions, sourced logs of the same diameter and coloration as the originals.

Over the years, the couple gutted and expanded the narrow galley kitchen, installing planed chestnut cabinets in a nod to the original construction. The screened-in porch was turned into a sitting room across the back of the house. A roughed-in area downstairs later became a guest suite. Other changes came gradually, among them a workout room, a new master bedroom wing, additional guest space, and closets, which the home had lacked.

Cozy or not, Tom and Toby didn't want the darkness to feel oppressive. They balanced the wood with generous swaths of fabric and wove a palette of soft reds and pale greens throughout. "Red is a great color for a cabin," Tom says. "It's very cheerful, and it helps reflect versus absorb light." Custom-made braided rugs and vintage hooked rugs warm the floors; lamps crafted from tea tins and old whisky barrels cast a gentle glow that makes the wood tones more luminous.

"It's all about comfort," Tom says. "It's such a welcoming house, and it would be even if it had nothing in it. It's just like an old shoe."

⌐ This rockwork fireplace was the only one in the cabin when Tom and Toby purchased it. As they added more fireplaces during renovations, they tried to stay as true as possible to its style and configuration.

› Twig furnishings create a sense of welcome at the home's entrance.

» Tom and Toby added the covered entry area, as well as the bridge and walkway that flank their hosta garden.

Strength of Spirit

Previous Overleaf: In the sunroom area, which once was a porch, 19th-century English oak furnishings lend an air of elegance that blends with the chestnut log walls. An English trout painting of the same era hangs above the mantel.

‹ In the living room, the walls tower nearly 20 feet high, unusual for a log home of the period. "In so many of Webb's cabins, you had eight- or nine-foot ceilings at the very maximum," Tom explains. "They didn't have tall ceilings because of keeping warm." The darkness of the logs preserves the sense of cabin snugness. "Sort of like a cozy womb," he says.

› At one end of the living room, a Black Forest clock that Tom and Toby wired as a lamp tops a 19th-century Spanish refectory table. Antique carved-antler candlesticks represent a play on traditional wall-hung antlers.

‹ The cabin's original staircase, built by local craftsman Joe Webb, overlooks the living room. Many of Webb's other cabins have gnarled rhododendron railings, says Tom, so the use of straight limbs is unusual.

⌃ Nineteenth-century English transferware surrounds a carved Black Forest mirror and an English dresser base, both of the same vintage. The red lamps were made by a North Georgia potter.

⌃ In the entry hall, which used to be a bedroom, Tom and Toby added a log Dutch door. A shed-antler sconce from England keeps company with an old wooden painted barrel, repurposed as a cane stand.

Strength of Spirit

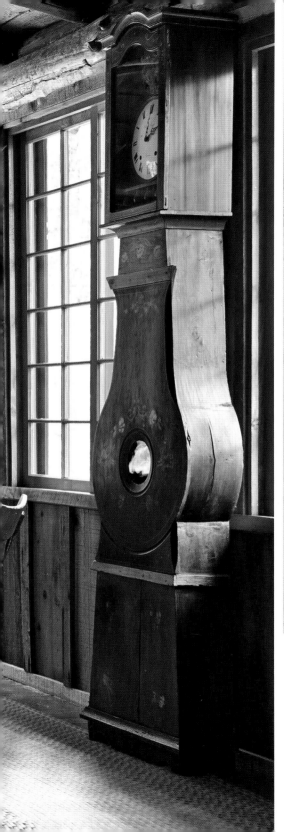

‹ A 19th-century French grandfather clock with a painted motif dominates the main dining area, anchored by a custom-braided rug.

⌃ Custom planed-chestnut cabinets replaced rudimentary versions in the kitchen, which was basic and dilapidated when Tom and Toby bought the house.

Strength of Spirit

∧ The guest suite on the terrace level looks out to the gardens, which inspired its green-and-white palette. Short curtains in the same Dutch-pattern toile as the headboard lighten the room's look and feel.

⌐ The painted bedside table was crafted by an Atlanta octogenarian, from whom Tom and Toby have commissioned multiple furnishings.

> Inviting toile armchairs flank a 19th-century English cricket table in the guest bedroom seating area.

≪ Tom and Toby added the master bedroom. A late 19th-century American patchwork quilt dresses the bed. In keeping with the home's original fireplace, the stonework on this new one combines two different styles: tidy on the bottom, random and askew from the mantel up.

‹ Like the terrace-level suite, the upstairs loft guestroom wears a green-and-white palette to blend with the foliage outside. The lamps are retrofitted English tole tea tins.

Strength of Spirit

˄ Tom and Toby added a garden area to the side of the house, complete with a stone fireplace.

˄ Although the garden area's twig fence is newly built, it looks as though it has been there since the cabin was built.

˄ This weathered bear statue, carved by a local woodcarver with a chainsaw, found a home amid Tom and Toby's hostas.

Strength of Spirit

RESOURCES

BORN TO BUILD

Braxton and Maryanna Dixon

3020 New Home Rd
Hendersonville, TN 37075
615.479.5481
todi7@comcast.net
Original Owner, William Oliver from Mudlick, KY
William Mongle, lead carpenter
Bobby and Billy Overstreet, disassembly and reassembly
    construction
David Shockley, transportation, Glascow, KY

CULTIVATING MEMORIES

Carolyn Malone Interiors

3277 Roswell Rd
Atlanta, GA 30305
404.264.9509
malonech@aol.com

Summershade Growing Trees

John Malone
3315 Old Monroe-Madison Hwy, NE
Madison, GA 30650
404.405.5805
malonejs@bellsouth.net
www.summershadegrowingtrees.com

The Malcolm Family

Neighbors who tirelessly helped resurrect the cabins with
    their craftsmanship and friendship.

DREAM HOME COME TRUE

Flynnside Out Productions, LLC

Brian Patrick Flynn
brian@flynnsideout.com
www.flynnsideout.com

Babcock Residential Group

General Contractor
www.babcockresidentialgroup.com

Custom Slipcover & Upholstery

www.slipuph.com

Grey Furniture

Stairwell, Custom Lighting and Mantel
www.greyfurniture.com

GROWING NEW ROOTS

D. Stanley Dixon Architect

2300 Peachtree Rd, NE, Suite C-101
Atlanta, GA 30309
404.574.1430
sdixon@dsdixonarchitect.com
www.dsdixonarchitect.com

Kathleen Rivers Interior Design

20 Atlantic St.
Charleston, SC 29401
828.743.6493
Kathleen@kathleenrivers.com
www.kathleenrivers.com

Rivers Residential, LLC

John Mears
2300 Peachtree Rd., Suite C-101
Atlanta, GA 30309
404.574.1433

A HASTY RETREAT

Kathleen Rivers Interior Design

20 Atlantic St
Charleston, SC 29401
828.743.6493
Kathleen@kathleenrivers.com
www.kathleenrivers.com

Dargan Landscape Architects/Dovecote

Hugh & Mary Palmer Dargan, RLAS
Cashiers & Atlanta, GA
828.743.0307
www.dargan.com

Jack Davis, Architect

2300 Peachtree Rd, NW, Suite B-203
Atlanta, GA 30309
404.237.2333
emailus@jackdavisarchitect.com
www.jackdavisarchitect.com

HISTORY AT HEART

J B Fuller Jr. Furniture Maker

J B Fuller
705 Cornelia Rd.
Brierfield, AL 35035
Jbfuller9@gmail.com

Evolutia

Robert Klinner, Reclaimed lumber
2850 35th Ave. North
Birmingham, AL 35234
www.evolutiamade.com

HOME IN THREE ACTS

FAIA Bonstra, Haresign Architects

David T. Haresign,
1728 14th St, NW, Suite-300
Washington, DC 20009
202.588.9373 (extension) 127
202.255.1611
dharesign@bonstra.com
www.bonstra.com

TimberBuilt Construction LLC

Greg Foster
516 Dearing Road
Flint Hill, VA 22627
540.675.3901
www.TimberBuiltConstruction.com

A Beautiful Earth

Teri Speight
7016 Foster St.
District Heights, MD 20747
cottageinthecourt@gmail.com
www.cottageinthecourt.com

Archway Stone Masonry

John Ward
2276 Saint David's Church Rd.
Fort Valley, VA 22652
540.933.6315
www.archwaystonemasonry.com

Rick's Custom Welding

Rick Nawrocki
113 Aileen Rd.
Flint Hill, VA 22627
540.675.1888
www.rickscustomwelding.com

Independent Air, Inc.

Chris Berta
5403 Sperryville Pike
Boston, VA 22713
540.987.8798
IndependentAir@hughes.net

HUNTING DOWN HISTORY

Spitzmiller and Norris, Inc.

Rick Spitzmiller and Robert Norris
349 Peachtree Hills Ave, Suite C-5
Atlanta, GA 30305
404.812.0224
mail@spitzmillerandnorris.com
www.spitzmillerandnorris.com

Dan DeKeyser Construction

Erika Reade, Ltd
3732 Roswell Rd NE, Atlanta, GA 30342
404.233.3857

LAID-BACK LUX

Charles Faudree, Inc., Interior Design
The business has been closed

Linda James Antiques

1345 E 15th St, Tulsa, OK 74120
918.295.7711
www.lindajamesantiques.com

Dearl Stewart Construction Company

P.O. Box 1364
Cashiers, NC 28721
704.743.2063

MIX MASTERED

Spitzmiller and Norris, Inc.

Rick Spitzmiller and Robert Norris
349 Peachtree Hills Ave, Suite C-5
Atlanta, GA 30305
404.812.0224
mail@spitzmillerandnorris.com
www.spitzmillerandnorris.com

Studio 21 Interiors

Laura Stearns
675 Pulaski St., Suite 2100
Athens GA 30601
706.474.6188
studio21interiors@gmail.com
www.studio21interiors.com

OLD CABIN NEW TRICKS

C. Weaks Interiors

Carole Weaks
349 Peachtree Hills Ave, NE, Suite B-4
Atlanta, GA 30305
404.233.6040
cweaksint@aol.com
www.cweaksint.com

STORIED PAST

Platt Architecture

Al Platt
33 West Main St.
Brevard, NC 28712
828.884.2393
info@plattarchitecture.com
www.plattarchitecture.com

Austin Interiors

Sherri Austin
5640 Errol Place NW
Atlanta, GA 30327
404.843.0218
sherri@austinenterprises.net

Bronco Construction, Inc.

Bob Dylewski
Ron Dickerson
4669 Boylston Hwy
Mills River, NC 28759
828.891.2782
www.broncoconstructioninc.com

STRENGTH OF SPIRIT

Toby West Antiques and Interior Design

P.O. Box 2007
341 Hwy 64 W, Suite 103/104
Cashiers, NC 28717
828.743.9117
Fax: 828.743.0935
info@tobywestantiques.com
Shop is seasonal April–November, Tues.–Sat. 10:00–5:00

Tom Chambers & Co. Builders LLC

Tommy Chambers
1359 Flat Mountain Rd.
Highlands, NC 28741
828.526.2075
Cell 828.421.0795
Fax 828.526.2522
tommychambers@tomchambers.com
www.tomchambersbuilders.com

Resources